General Knowledge Olympiad

Class 03

A must have book for all Olympiads & Talent Search Exams...

by
Deepak Sharma

BLOOM CAP
Bloom Cap Edu Ventures Pvt. Ltd.

Bloom Cap Edu Ventures Pvt. Ltd.

卐 **© Publisher**

No part of this publication may be re-produced, stored in a retrieval system or by any means, electronic, mechanical, photocopying, recording, scanning, web or otherwise without the written permission of the publisher. Publisher has obtained all the information in this book from the sources believed to be reliable and true. However, Publisher or its editors or authors or illustrators don't take any responsibility for the absolute accuracy of any information published and the damage or loss suffered thereupon.

All disputes subject to Delhi jurisdiction only.

卐 **Administrative & Production Office**

'Ramchhaya' 4577/15, Agarwal Road, Darya Ganj, New Delhi -110002
Tele: 011- 47630600, 43518550

卐 **ISBN :** 978-93-25519-42-8

卐 **PRICE :** ₹100.00

卐 **PO No :** TXT-XX-XXXXXXX-X-XX

For further information about the books log on to
www.bloomcap.org

Follow us on   

Preface

"Future belongs to those Who prepares for it today"

School Olympiads are National & International level competitions conducted by different Government, Non-Government & Educational Organisations with the purpose of making the children ready to face competitive exams.

The challenging Questions asked in Olympiads motivate them to learn more & more and bring out the best result with improved academic performance. The Awards & Scholarship offered by Olympiads motivate children to aspire & strive for doing better and emerge out to be the best.

GK Olympiads

GK is the knowledge of every aspect of the human life, which may or may not be the part of routine academic studies but very important for the overall personality development of the students. It is more or less connected with the attentiveness and awareness. There can be different domains of GK like; History, Geography, Polity, Culture, Discovery, Sports, Current Affairs etc.

GK Olympiads help students in understanding the importance of General Knowledge and updations about National & International Affairs in daily life..

'Bloom GK Olympiad Study Book Class 3' is a perfect resource to Study & Practice for Olympiad Exams and other National & State Level Talent Search Exams & Other Competitions.

Some Special Features of Bloom GK Olympiad Study Books are;

- Complete coverage of all the topics related to GK;. Geography, Polity, Sports, Current Affairs etc.
- Chapterwise Exercises having different types of Objective Questions.
- Olympiad Pattern Practice Sets at the end.

This book is prepared by Expert Panel with the utmost care, still if you have any suggestions regarding its improvement then feel free to contact us at olympiads@bloomcap.org. We will try to inculcate your suggestions in the further editions.

Contents

Chapter 01

Solar System

1. Which planet has very cold temperatures on it?
   (a) Mercury
   (b) Earth
   (c) Mars
   (d) Neptune

2. How many planets are there in our Solar System?
   (a) 9
   (b) 6
   (c) 7
   (d) 8

3. What is the correct arrangement of the planets from Sun in the options given below?
   (a) Mercury, Venus, Mars, Earth
   (b) Mercury, Saturn, Venus, Earth
   (c) Mercury, Venus, Earth, Mars
   (d) Venus, Mars, Mercury, Saturn

4. What constitutes the Solar System?
   (a) Sun
   (b) Mars
   (c) Moon
   (d) All of these

5. What is Sun?
   (a) A Planet
   (b) A Galaxy
   (c) A Star
   (d) A Comet

6. Pick the odd one out :
   (a) Gases
   (b) Comets
   (c) Planets
   (d) Asteroids

7. Pick out the odd one out from the following options.

   (**Hint**: stars have their own light)
   (a) Earth
   (b) Mars
   (c) Jupiter
   (d) Sun

8. Earth is the .... planet in our solar system.
   (a) fifth
   (b) second
   (c) fourth
   (d) third

9. Name the planet shown in given image.

(a) Earth   (b) Venus
(c) Mars   (d) Saturn

10. On the basis of facts some statements given below are true or false, find the correct sequence.

A. Earth is known as blue planet.
B. Jupiter is the smallest planet in our solar system.

(a) A-False, B-True   (b) A-True, B-False
(c) A-True, B-False   (d) None of these

11. The 'Blue planet' is located in the solar system between which two planets?

(a) Mercury and Venus   (b) Venus and Mars
(c) Mars and Jupiter   (d) Jupiter and Neptune

12. Which of these planet is made up of gases?

(a) Mars   (b) Mercury
(c) Saturn   (d) Earth

13. Name the largest planet in our Solar System.

(a) Earth   (b) Saturn
(c) Jupiter   (d) Mars

14. Which out of the following is not the part of our Solar System?

(a) Mars   (b) Earth
(c) Pluto   (d) Neptune

15. The floating rock pieces in the outer space are known as ....

(a) Comet   (b) Meteor
(c) Asteroid   (d) Planets

16. .... and .... are known as the nearest neighbours of Earth.

(a) Jupiter, Saturn   (b) Mercury, Venus
(c) Neptune, Uranus   (d) Jupiter, Venus

17. Tailed stars are known as........... .

   (a) Comets   (b) Planets
   (c) Sun   (d) Moon

18. Which planet is similar to Earth in its shape and size?
   (a) Mars   (b) Jupiter
   (c) Venus   (d) Uranus

19. The complete rotation of Earth on its own axis is known as........... .
   (a) one year   (b) one month
   (c) one day   (d) None of these

20. Read the statements and select the correct option.
   A. Moon looks white because it has its own light.
   B. All planets get light from the Sun.
   Codes
   (a) A is correct   (b) B is correct
   (c) Both are correct   (d) None are correct

21. .... is known as the blue planet.
   (a) Mars   (b) Jupiter
   (c) Neptune   (d) Earth

22. Which planet can be seen in the sky during evening?
   (a) Mars   (b) Jupiter   (c) Venus   (d) Neptune

23. Which one revolves around the Earth?
   (a) Sun   (b) Moon
   (c) Stars   (d) All of these

24. The Earth completes one revolution in............ .
   (a) 30 days   (b) 365 days
   (c) 1 day   (d) 27 days

25. Stars give out.
   (a) Only heat   (b) Only light
   (c) Both heat and light   (d) None of these

26. The energy captured from Sun is known as ....
    (a) wind energy   (b) solar energy
    (c) nuclear energy   (d) electrical energy

27. Which planet in the solar system has only one natural satellite?
    (a) Mars   (b) Neptune
    (c) Jupiter   (d) Earth

28. Which is known as the natural satellite of Earth?
    (a) Moon   (b) Sun
    (c) Stars   (d) None of these

29. Earth receives heat and light from the ....
    (a) Moon   (b) Mars
    (c) Jupiter   (d) Sun

30. How much time is taken by Sun rays to reach to the Earth's surface?
    (a) 8 minutes   (b) 7 minutes
    (c) 6 minutes   (d) None of these

31. Which objects in the sky have their own light?
    A. Sun   B. Stars   C Planets
    (a) A and C   (b) A and B
    (c) B and C   (d) A, B, C

32. Which planet is known as the 'morning star'?
    (a) Jupiter   (b) Venus
    (c) Mars   (d) None of these

33. How many 'Gas Giant' planets are there in our solar system?
    (a) Six   (b) Four
    (c) Two   (d) Eight

34. Moon cannot take the shape of
    (a)   (b)   (c)   (d)

Chapter 02

My Country

1. India is located in which continent?
   (a) Europe
   (b) Asia
   (c) Australia
   (d) Antarctica

2. India shares its land border with which country?
   (a) United States of America
   (b) United Kingdom
   (c) Japan
   (d) China

3. Which of the following is not the neighbouring country of India?
   (a) Nepal
   (b) Bhutan
   (c) Pakistan
   (d) Australia

4. Name the largest state of our country.
   (a) Haryana
   (b) Gujarat
   (c) Manipur
   (d) Rajasthan

5. Thar desert is located in India in which state?
   (a) Uttar Pradesh
   (b) Rajasthan
   (c) Haryana
   (d) Odisha

6. Pick the odd one out from the following options.
   (a) Daman and Diu
   (b) Ladakh
   (c) Andaman and Nicobar Islands
   (d) Uttar Pradesh

7. Which of the following set of states have same capital?
   (a) Rajasthan-Gujarat
   (b) Uttar Pradesh-Uttarakhand
   (c) Punjab-Haryana
   (d) Manipur-Assam

8. National river of India is........... .
   (a) Indus
   (b) Ganga
   (c) Brahmaputra
   (d) Krishna

9. Match the following.

List I	List II
A. Sun Temple	1. Punjab
B. Golden Temple	2. Odisha
C. Badrinath Temple	3. Madhya Pradesh
D. Mahakaleshwar Jyotirlinga	4. Uttarakhand

Codes

	A	B	C	D			A	B	C	D
(a)	3	2	4	1		(b)	2	1	3	4
(c)	2	1	4	3		(d)	None of these			

10. Which of these Union Territory is surrounded by ocean?
    (a) Ladakh   (b) Delhi
    (c) Lakshadweep   (d) Chandigarh

11. Match the following.

List I	List II
A. Maharashtra	1. Dispur
B. Gujarat	2. Gandhinagar
C. Assam	3. Mumbai
D. Rajasthan	4. Jaipur

Codes

	A	B	C	D			A	B	C	D
(a)	2	3	1	4		(b)	3	2	1	4
(c)	4	3	1	2		(d)	None of these			

12. Which of the pairs given below is not true?
    (a) Uttar Pradesh-Lucknow   (b) Uttarakhand-Dehradun
    (c) Rajasthan-Jaipur   (d) Madhya Pradesh-Agartala

13. Which of the following is the smallest Union Territory in terms of area?
    (a) Delhi   (b) Andaman and Nicobar Islands
    (c) Chandigarh   (d) Lakshadweep

14. 'Vande Mataram' is known as the......... .
    (a) National Anthem   (b) National Music
    (c) National Song   (d) None of these

15. Match the following.

	List I	List II
A.	Punjab	1. Chhath Puja
B.	Bihar	2. Pongal
C.	Kolkata	3. Baisakhi
D.	Tamil Nadu	4. Durga Puja

Codes

	A	B	C	D			A	B	C	D
(a)	1	3	4	2		(b)	3	2	4	1
(c)	3	1	4	2		(d)	None of these			

16. Bohag Bihu is celebrated in which of the following states?
(a) Assam
(b) Haryana
(c) Arunachal Pradesh
(d) Andhra Pradesh

17. Which of the following famous site is located in Punjab?
(a) Hawa Mahal
(b) Somnath Temple
(c) Golden Temple
(d) Sun Temple

18. White colour in the National Flag of India represents........... .
(a) peace and truth
(b) strength and courage
(c) growth and auspiciousness of the land
(d) None of these

19. Match the following.

	List I	List II
A.	Maharashtra	1. Rice Dish
B.	Assam	2. Idli and Sambar
C.	Tamil Nadu	3. Vada Pav

Codes

	A	B	C			A	B	C
(a)	1	2	3		(b)	2	3	1
(c)	2	1	3		(d)	3	1	2

20. Which of the following state celebrates Lohri?
(a) Gujarat
(b) Maharashtra
(c) Bihar
(d) Punjab

Countries of the World

1. Name the capital of United States of America.
   (a) Paris
   (b) London
   (c) New Zealand
   (d) Washington DC

2. Match the following.

Country		Capital
A. United Kingdom	1.	London
B. France	2.	Islamabad
C. Pakistan	3.	Paris

Codes

	A	B	C		A	B	C
(a)	1	3	2	(b)	3	1	2
(c)	2	1	3	(d) None of these		

3. Name the currency shown in the image.

   (a) Dollar
   (b) Dinar
   (c) Rupees
   (d) None of these

4. Name the largest country in the world (in terms of area).
   (a) Germany
   (b) China
   (c) Russia
   (d) India

5. "I am the second largest country in the world (in terms of population)", what is my name?
   (a) New Zealand
   (b) Australia
   (c) America
   (d) India

6. Tokyo is the capital of which country?
   (a) India
   (b) Singapore
   (c) Japan
   (d) Russia

7. Name the capital of Nepal.
   (a) Delhi
   (b) Islamabad
   (c) Tokyo
   (d) Kathmandu

8. Riyal is the currency of which country?
   (a) USA
   (b) Saudi Arabia
   (c) India
   (d) Russia

9. Name the country whose flag is shown in the image.

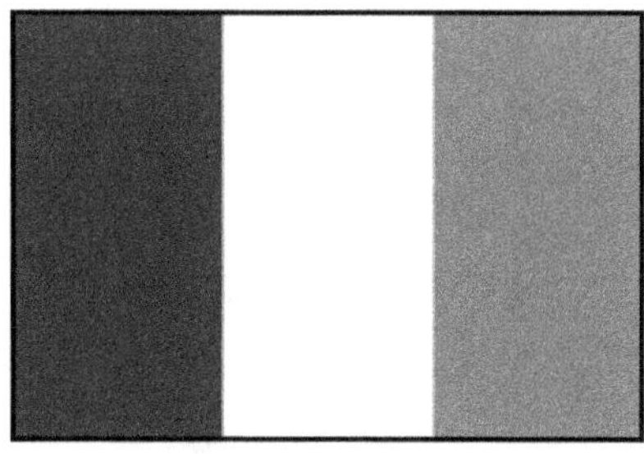

   (a) Australia
   (b) Germany
   (c) France
   (d) India

10. Kabul is the capital of which country?
    (a) Bangladesh
    (b) India
    (c) Afghanistan
    (d) Iran

11. Identify the name of the country from the given flag.

    (a) Sri Lanka
    (b) India
    (c) Russia
    (d) Japan

12. 'Moscow' is the capital of which country?
    (a) America   (b) Russia
    (c) United Kingdom   (d) Japan

13. Which of the following is the currency of Japan?
    (a) Yen   (b) Dollar
    (c) Pound   (d) Dinar

14. .... is the capital of China.
    (a) Delhi   (b) Hong Kong
    (c) Dubai   (d) Beijing

15. Rome is the capital of which country in the world?
    (a) Singapore   (b) Pakistan
    (c) Turkey   (d) Italy

16. Name the currency shown in the image.

    (a) Pound   (b) Dollar
    (c) Dinar   (d) Euro

17. Identify the name of the country from the given flag.

    (a) Pakistan   (b) China
    (c) America   (d) Iraq

18. Baghdad is the capital of which country?
    (a) Russia   (b) India
    (c) China   (d) Iraq

19. Name the currency shown in the image.

(a) Rupee   (b) Dollar   (c) Dinar   (d) Pound

20. Identify the name of the country from the given flag.

(a) Nepal   (b) China
(c) Pakistan   (d) Myanmar

21. Name the currency shown in the image.

(a) Pound   (b) Dollar
(c) Rupees   (d) None of these

22. Identify the name of the country from the given flag.

Hint It is our neighbouring country
(a) Pakistan   (b) Russia
(c) Bhutan   (d) Japan

23. Identify the name of the country from the given flag.

(a) America   (b) Russia
(c) Bangladesh   (d) Pakistan

24. Check the image below and identify the country.

Hint: The Walt Disney World is situated in this country.
(a) India   (b) United States of America
(c) Pakistan   (d) Russia

25. Name the country whose flag is shown in the image.

(a) China   (b) Russia
(c) Japan   (d) India

26. The image shown is the currency of which country?

(a) India   (b) Dubai
(c) Pakistan   (d) Bangladesh

27. Name the country from the image given below that is known for its natural wonders.

Hint: The Great Barrier Reef and Sydney Opera House is located in this country.
(a) Russia   (b) India
(c) China   (d) Australia

28. Identify the name of the country from the given flag.

(a) Italy   (b) Japan
(c) America   (d) United Kingdom

Music and Dance

1. Which of the following is a 'classical' dance form?
   (a) Kalaripayattu
   (b) Chhobia
   (c) Bhawai
   (d) Kathakali

2. This semi classical Indian dance originated in Eastern India which is performed by wearing a mask. It is a blend of martial and tribal art forms and based on folk traditions of India. Mention the name of this dance.

   (a) Kathak
   (b) Bharatanatyam
   (c) Chhau Dance
   (d) Gaudiya Nritya

3. Koodiyattam is a............ .
   (a) traditional dance of Kerala
   (b) special food prepared in Tamil Nadu
   (c) boat race of Kerala
   (d) dress worn in Karnataka

4. How many 'Sur' are there in music?
   (a) 8
   (b) 9
   (c) 10
   (d) 7

5. Which of the following is not the Indian traditional dance?
   (a) Bharatanatyam
   (b) Kathakali
   (c) Kathak
   (d) Salsa

6. Name the most traditional classical dance art of India that originated in Kerala and is mentioned in Natya Shastra.

(a) Bharatanatyam	(b) Chhau Dance
(c) Kathakali	(d) Sattriya

7. Kuchipudi is a dance drama of which of the following states?
(a) Andhra Pradesh   (b) Kerala
(c) Karnataka   (d) Tamil Nadu

8. Which of the following is not correctly matched?
(a) Ravi Shankar - Sitarist   (b) M.F Hussain - Tabla
(c) R.K Narayan - Novelist   (d) Kaifi Azmi - Poet

9. With which of the following instruments is Anuradha Pal associated?
(a) Sitar   (b) Veena   (c) Tabla   (d) Mandolin

10. The MohiniAttam dance form was developed in ....
(a) Andhra Pradesh   (b)Karnataka
(c) Kerala   (d) Tamil Nadu

11. .... is an Indian classical dance form that is found in three distinct forms of gharanas – Banaras, Jaipur and Lucknow.

(a) Kathak   (b) Sattriya   (c) Kuchipudi   (d) Odissi

12. Identify the singer shown in the image.

   (a) Shaan   (b) Sonu Nigam
   (c) Himesh Reshammiya   (d) Arijit Singh

13. Which dance form is shown in the given image?

   (a) Kathakali   (b) Bharatanatyam
   (c) Kuchipudi   (d) Salsa

14. Which of the following is not the Indian traditional dance?
   (a) Bharatanatyam   (b) Kathakali
   (c) Kathak   (d) Salsa

15. Garba is related to which of the following festivals?
   (a) Navratri   (b) Holi or Diwali
   (c) Pongal   (d) Baisakhi

16. Which of these is a wind instrument?
   (a) Sitar   (b) Shehnai
   (c) Pakhawaj   (d) Mridangam

17. Identify the famous Kathak Dancer.

   (a) S P Balasubramaniam   (b) Birju Maharaj
   (c) Uday Shankar   (d) Udit Narayan

18. Which of the following musical instruments is of Indian origin?
   (a) Guitar   (b) Drums
   (c) Piano   (d) Flute

19. Which playback singer has been awarded the Bharat Ratna, the nation's highest civilian honour?
   (a) Ustad Ali Akbar Khan   (b) Sonu Nigam
   (c) Udit Narayan   (d) Lata Mangeshkar

20. The oldest form of composition of Hindustani Vocal Music is ....
   (a) Ghazal   (b) Dhrupad
   (c) Thumri   (d) Qawwali

21. Name the Indian Musician who had received Oscar as well as Grammy Award.
   (a) A.R Rahman   (b) Hariprasad Chaurasia
   (c) Zakir Hussain   (d) None of these

Chapter 05

Transport and Communication

1. Fastest means of transport is ....
   (a) Aeroplane
   (b) Ship
   (c) Bus
   (d) Train

2. The transfer of information and ideas from one person to another is called ....
   (a) Social communication
   (b) Digital communication
   (c) Personal communication
   (d) Mass communication

3. .... is an example of water transport and .... is an example of air transport.
   (a) Ship, truck
   (b) Bus, aeroplane
   (c) Ship, helicopter
   (d) None of these

4. Places located on the coast have .... to anchor ships.
   (a) harbours
   (b) railway track
   (c) bus stop
   (d) airport

5. Pick the odd one out.
   (a) Shatabdi Express
   (b) Rajdhani Express
   (c) Nauchandi Express
   (d) Expressways

6. Which animal can be used as a means of transport?
   (a) Camel
   (b) Bull
   (c) Horse
   (d) All of these

7. Find the wrong match from the following options.
   (a) Water Transport – Cargo Ship
   (b) Air Transport   – Helicopters
   (c) Land Transport   – Bike
   (d) Rail Transport   – Boeing 747

8. .... is the fastest way to send a message.
   (a) Postcard
   (b) Speed Post
   (c) Telegram
   (d) E-mail

9. Which of these is a means of mass communication?
   (a) Internet
   (b) Newspaper
   (c) Television
   (d) All of these

10. Which out of the following is not a means of communication?
    (a) Mobile
    (b) Internet
    (c) Postcard
    (d) Bulb

11. Name the biggest international airport in India.
(a) Indira Gandhi International Airport.
(b) Netaji Subhash Chandra Bose International Airport, Kolkata.
(c) Chennai International Airport, Chennai.
(d) Thiruvananthapuram International Airport.

12. Which of the following is not a personal communication?
(a) Letters (b) Telephone (c) E-mail (d) Newspaper

13. What is the world ranking of Indian Railway network?
(a) 1st (b) 2nd (c) 3rd (d) 4th

14. Which type of transport can move over only a fixed path?
(a) Road Transport (b) Water Transport
(c) Rail Transport (d) Air Transport

15. Among the given options which one is the slowest mode of transport?
(a) Bicycle (b) Bus
(c) Bullock cart (d) Cargo Ship

16. You can chat with your friend through........... .
(a) Landline phone (b) Internet
(c) Printer (d) Fax

17. 'SMS' stands for ....
(a) Short Message Service (b) Site Message Service
(c) Self Message Service (d) None of these

18. The first Indian passenger train ran between .... and ....
(a) Delhi, Mumbai (b) Agra, Kanpur
(c) Bori Bunder, Thane (d) None of these

19. Which of the following is not a means of land transport?
(a) Scooter (b) Truck (c) Car (d) Boat

20. Which of the following is a form of Tele-communication?
(a) Post Card (b) Radio (c) Magazine (d) Newspaper

21. Ram lives in Delhi, his cousin lives in Australia, If Ram wants to send a gift to his cousin, which means of transport should he use?
(a) Bus (b) Train
(c) Airplane (d) Metro

22. When there was no mobile and internet, people sent messages to each other through which means?
(a) Railways (b) Pigeons
(c) Motorbikes (d) Bullock carts

Chapter 06

Famous Places

1. Gateway of India is situated in which city?
(a) Mumbai
(b) Jaipur
(c) Udaipur
(d) Delhi

2. The Parliament of India is located at ....
(a) Delhi
(b) Jaipur
(c) Agra
(d) Mathura

3. Which city is known as the 'City of Lakes'?
(a) Konark
(b) Udaipur
(c) Mumbai
(d) Jaipur

4. Identify the popular railway station shown in the picture.

(a) New Delhi Railway Station
(b) Chattrapati Shivaji Terminal
(c) Howrah Railway Station
(d) Jaisalmer Railway Terminal

5. Name the place where 'Taj Mahal' is situated.
(a) Delhi
(b) Agra
(c) Hyderabad
(d) None of these

6. Name the tallest statue of India.
(a) Statue of Liberty
(b) Statue of M.K. Gandhi
(c) Statue of Indira Gandhi
(d) Statue of Unity

7. Which Indian city is known as the 'Golden City'?
(a) Udaipur
(b) Rampur
(c) Jaisalmer
(d) Hyderabad

8. Name the place where Republic Day parade takes place.
(a) Agra
(b) Red Fort
(c) Rajpath
(d) None of these

9. Which city of India is known as Orange City?
(a) Jaipur
(b) Meerut
(c) Nagpur
(d) Delhi

10. The Buddha Statue shown in the image is located in which state?

(a) Bihar
(b) Uttar Pradesh
(c) Maharashtra
(d) Odisha

11. India Gate is located in which city of India?
(a) Mumbai
(b) Delhi
(c) Agra
(d) Meerut

12. Which temple is also known as 'Harmandir Sahib Temple'?
(a) Sun Temple
(b) Golden Temple
(c) Agra Mahal
(d) None of these

13. Name the city where Supreme Court of India is situated.
(a) Jaipur
(b) Rampur
(c) Jamnagar
(d) Delhi

14. Name the city where 'Howrah Bridge' is situated.
(a) Delhi
(b) Mumbai
(c) West Bengal
(d) None of these

15. Tick the option (place) where, Kumbh Mela is not held or organised.
(a) Agra
(b) Ujjain
(c) Haridwar
(d) Nashik

16. 'Rock Garden' is located in ....
(a) Delhi
(b) Himachal Pradesh
(c) Punjab
(d) Chandigarh

17. Name the place where 'Rashtrapati Bhavan' is located.
(a) Jamnagar
(b) Patna
(c) Delhi
(d) Ramnagar

18. Which city of India is known as 'City of Sat Tal' (7 lakes)?
    (a) Nainital   (b) Shimla
    (c) Delhi   (d) Haryana

19. Name the place where 'Char Minar' is situated.
    (a) Delhi   (b) Hyderabad
    (c) Shimla   (d) Meerut

20. Name the highest mountain peak of the world.
    (a) Mount Everest   (b) Kangchenjunga
    (c) Dhaulagiri   (d) None of these

21. The tower shown in the image is popularly known as.............. .

    (a) Big Ben Tower   (b) Eiffel Tower
    (c) Leaning Tower of Pisa   (d) None of these

22. Name the city, where Burj Khalifa is located.
    (a) Dubai   (b) New York
    (c) London   (d) Beijing

23. In which country world's longest manmade structure is located?
    (a) China   (b) India
    (c) Australia   (d) Russia

24. The tower shown in the image is known as.............. .

    (a) Leaning Tower of Pisa   (b) Eiffel Tower
    (c) Big Ben Tower   (d) None of these

National Personalities

1. Who was the first woman Prime Minister of India?
   (a) Sarojini Naidu
   (b) Indira Gandhi
   (c) Nirmala Sitaraman
   (d) Sonia Gandhi

2. Who was the first President of India?
   (a) Rajendra Prasad
   (b) C.V. Raman
   (c) S. Radhakrishnan
   (d) Jawaharlal Nehru

3. Name the first woman President of India?
   (a) Kiran Bedi
   (b) Kiran Majumdar Shaw
   (c) Pratibha Patil
   (d) Sonia Gandhi

4. What is the nickname given to personality shown in the picture?

   (a) Iron Man of India
   (b) Missile Man of India
   (c) Water Man of India
   (d) Food Man of India

5. Who among the following gave the slogan 'Jai Jawan Jai Kisan'?
   (a) Jawaharlal Nehru
   (b) Lal Bahadur Shastri
   (c) Deen Dayal Upadhyay
   (d) Mahatma Gandhi

6. Who was the first Prime Minister of India?
   (a) Jawaharlal Nehru
   (b) Lal Bahadur Shastri
   (c) Ram Dhari Singh Dinkar
   (d) None of these

7. Who among the following gave the slogan 'Do or Die'?
   (a) Mahatma Gandhi
   (b) Lal Bahadur Shastri
   (c) Sardar Patel
   (d) Harivansh Rai Bachchan

8. Who among the following gave the slogan 'Inquilab Zindabad'?
   (a) Bhagat Singh
   (b) Mangal Pandey
   (c) Lal Bahadur Shastri
   (d) None of these

9. Who among the following is known as the 'Iron Man of India'?
   (a) M.K. Gandhi
   (b) Vallabhbhai Patel
   (c) Narendra Modi
   (d) None of these

10. Who is the inventor of bulb?
    (a) Albert Einstein
    (b) Newton
    (c) Thomas Alva Edison
    (d) C.V. Raman

11. Identify the personality shown in the picture.
    Hint: He wrote our National Anthem

    (a) Bankim Chandra Chatterjee
    (b) Subhash Chandra Bose
    (c) Rabindra Nath Tagore
    (d) Deen Dayal Upadhayay

12. Who among the following is known as the 'Nightingale of India'?
    (a) Lata Mangeshkar
    (b) Sarojini Naidu
    (c) Sunidhi Chauhan
    (d) Asha Bhosle

13. Name the first guru of 'Sikhs'.
    (a) Guru Gobind Singh ji
    (b) Guru Tegh Bahadur ji
    (c) Guru Nanak Dev ji
    (d) None of these

14. Who was the first Indian to travel in space?
    (a) Rakesh Sharma
    (b) Kalpana Chawla
    (c) Neil Armstrong
    (d) None of these

15. Who among the following is known as the 'Master Blaster'?
    (a) Virat Kohli   (b) Rohit Sharma
    (c) MS Dhoni   (d) Sachin Tendulkar

16. Who is the richest person of India?
    (a) Jeff Bezos   (b) Elon Musk
    (c) Bill Gates   (d) Mukesh Ambani

17. Identify the personality shown in the image.

    (a) Priyanka Chopra   (b) Hima Das
    (c) Kalpana Chawla   (d) PT Usha

18. Identify the person shown in the image.

    (a) Satyanarayana Murthy   (b) Anand Mahindra
    (c) Ratan Tata   (d) None of these

19. Name the Indian mathematician, who is popularly known as 'Human Computer'.
    (a) Shakuntala Devi   (b) Ramanujan
    (c) Albert Einstein   (d) Uma Kapila

Chapter 08

Human Body

1. Digested food is absorbed and transported in the body by ....
   (a) blood   (b) mouth   (c) lungs   (d) water

2. Two or more bones are connected at.............. .
   (a) muscles   (b) tissues   (c) joints   (d) organs

3. Our heart has .... chambers.
   (a) one   (b) two   (c) four   (d) three

4. The bone that protects the brain is called ....
   (a) skull   (b) spine
   (c) ribcage   (d) None of these

5. Find the incorrect statement.
   (a) We breathe faster when we run.   (b) Kidneys are located in our skull.
   (c) We have two eyes.   (d) All of these

6. Select the odd one out.
   (a) Mouth   (b) Kidney
   (c) Pancreas   (d) Small Intestine

7. The organ shown in the image is ....

   (a) Brain   (b) Lungs   (c) Kidneys   (d) Heart

8. Which of the following is the main coordinating and controlling centre of the body?
   (a) Heart
   (b) Brain
   (c) Stomach
   (d) Nerves

9. What 'R' and 'W' stands for in RBC and WBC?
   (a) Red and Wright
   (b) Round and White
   (c) Red and White
   (d) None of these

10. Which is the smallest bone of human body?
    (a) Stapes (bone of ear)
    (b) Skull
    (c) Ribs
    (d) Femur

11. Identify our body system by which the waste material is removed from the body.
    (a) Circulatory System
    (b) Nervous System
    (c) Skeletal System
    (d) Excretory System

12. The .... is an organ that helps to digest food.
    (a) lungs
    (b) kidney
    (c) brain
    (d) stomach

13. We have .... kidneys.
    (a) 2
    (b) 1
    (c) 3
    (d) 4

14. Which of the following controls all our activities of seeing, hearing, learning, thinking and feeling?
    (a) Skeletal System
    (b) Nervous System
    (c) Excretory System
    (d) Circulatory System

15. Which is the longest bone of human body?
    (a) Stapes
    (b) Femur
    (c) Ribs
    (d) None of these

16. The voice box help us to speak, make sounds and sing. Where is it found?
    (a) Rib
    (b) Heart
    (c) Lungs
    (d) Throat

17. Name the gas which comes out of our body when we exhale.
    (a) Oxygen
    (b) Nitrogen
    (c) Sulphur
    (d) Carbon Dioxide

18. The system which helps us in taking food and making it ready for use by the body is......... .
    (a) digestive system
    (b) circulatory system
    (c) reproductive system
    (d) muscular system

19. Which of the following systems gives shape to our body?
    (a) Muscular System
    (b) Nervous System
    (c) Skeletal System
    (d) Circulatory System

20. Which of the following body parts are called 'Gateways of Knowledge'?
    (a) Body Systems   (b) Sense Organs
    (c) Legs   (d) Hands

21. The number of muscles present in our body are ....
    (a) 106   (b) 206   (c) 600   (d) 700

22. Brain, spinal cord and nerves are part of ....
    (a) circulatory system   (b) nervous system
    (c) respiratory system   (d) excretory system

23. .... are the smallest unit of our body.
    (a) Protein   (b) Vitamin   (c) Cells/Cell   (d) None of these

24. Which system of human body keep us to tealk, talk, lift and chew?
    (a) Nervous System   (b) Skeletal System
    (c) Muscular System   (d) Digestive System

25. Name the organ shown in the diagram.

    (a) Heart   (b) Brain   (c) Lungs   (d) None of these

26. Human blood is red due to presence of .... in the blood.
    (a) RBC   (b) WBC
    (c) Plasma   (d) None of these

27. .... is a watery substance that is present in our mouth and it makes food soft.
    (a) Teeth   (b) Tongue   (c) Saliva   (d) None of these

28. How does blood travel through the body?
    (a) Through the spine   (b) Through tubes called vessels
    (c) Through the intestines   (d) None of these

29. Headache, migraine and tumour are the problems of .... system.
    (a) digestive   (b) nervous   (c) reproductive   (d) muscular

30. Identify the name of the organs of digestive system.
    (a) Stomach   (b) Mouth
    (c) Small Intestine   (d) All of these

Chapter 09

Food and Nutrition

1. Potatoes, cereals, beans, pulses and oats are rich in ....
   (a) proteins
   (b) vitamins
   (c) minerals
   (d) carbohydrates

2. We consume milk in many ways. Which of these items does not come from milk?
   (a) Curd
   (b) Cream
   (c) Butter
   (d) Cereal

3. Which of the following food components does not provide any nutrients?
   (a) Milk
   (b) Water
   (c) Fruit juice
   (d) Vegetable soup

4. Milk and dairy products are rich in ....
   (a) proteins
   (b) fats
   (c) calcium
   (d) Both (a) and (c)

5. Which of the following food products are the best sources of animal proteins?
   (a) Milk
   (b) Egg
   (c) Cheese
   (d) All of these

6. Which of the following food components are called protective foods or micronutrients?
   (a) Carbohydrates
   (b) Proteins
   (c) Fats
   (d) Vitamins and minerals

7. Food stuffs containing 'fats' and 'carbohydrates' are called ....
   (a) body building foods
   (b) protective foods
   (c) energy giving foods
   (d) None of these

8. Pick the odd one out.
   (a) Clove
   (b) Chickpea
   (c) Turmeric
   (d) Cumin

9. Orange and Lemon is a good source of ....
   (a) Vitamin A
   (b) Vitamin D
   (c) Vitamin C
   (d) Vitamin B12

10. 'Sunlight' is a good source of which vitamin?
    (a) Vitamin A
    (b) Vitamin B12
    (c) Vitamin D
    (d) Vitamin E

11. Lack of which vitamin in our body will result in weak vision?
    (a) Vitamin D
    (b) Vitamin A
    (c) Vitamin C
    (d) Vitamin K

12. Which of the following components are major nutrients in our food?
    (a) Carbohydrates
    (b) Lipids and Proteins
    (c) Vitamins and Minerals
    (d) All of these

13. .... is a mineral that is vital for building strong bones and teeth.
    (a) Calcium
    (b) Iron
    (c) Magnesium
    (d) Potassium

14. Milk, cheese, and yogurt are in which group?
    (a) Meat group
    (b) Dairy group
    (c) Bread group
    (d) None of these

15. Which of the following vitamin is required to keep our bones strong?
    (a) Vitamin C
    (b) Vitamin D
    (c) Vitamin K
    (d) Vitamin B

16. Eating too much sugar is the leading cause for what diseases?
    (a) Common cold
    (b) Diabetes
    (c) The flu
    (d) Obesity

17. Which of the following is a good source of protein?
    (a) Pulses
    (b) Eggs
    (c) Chicken
    (d) All of these

18. Which of the following methods is incorrect to preserve food materials?
    (a) Keeping the food at low temperature.
    (b) Keeping the food in air tight container
    (c) Salting and sugaring.
    (d) Keeping it in water and room temperature.

19. Which oil is used for cooking in South India?
    (a) Coconut oil
    (b) Sunflower oil
    (c) Olive oil
    (d) None of these

20. Which vitamins are rich in carrots?
    (a) Vitamin A
    (b) Vitamin K
    (c) Vitamin B6
    (d) All of these

21. As rice is related to cereals in the same way groundnut is related to ....
    (a) pulses
    (b) cereals
    (c) oil seeds
    (d) milk products

Chapter 10

Everyday Science

1. What is found on the grass and flowers early in the morning?
   (a) Dew   (b) Fog   (c) Dust   (d) Ice

2. Why does a hydrogen balloon rises in the air?
   (a) Because it is lighter than the body of the air which it displaces.
   (b) Because it is heavier than the body of the air which it displaces.
   (c) Because it has bigger shape than air.
   (d) All of the above

3. Out of the following things,which is made by man?
   (a) Plastic   (b) Petroleum   (c) Coal   (d) Wood

4. Why does an electrician wear rubber gloves?
   (a) Because rubber partially allow electricity to pass through it.
   (b) Because rubber allow electricity to pass through it.
   (c) Because rubber does not allow electricity to pass through it.
   (d) None of the above

5. Identify the solid among the following.
   (a) Milk   (b) Water   (c) Ice   (d) Cold drink

6. 'LPG' stands for ....
   (a) Liquefied Petroleum Gas   (b) Liqued Petroleum Gas
   (c) Liquified Petrol Gas   (d) Light Petroleum Gas

7. Dark rain clouds can give out lightning and ....
   (a) thunder   (b) snow   (c) sunlight   (d) wind

8. What is the boiling point of water?
   (a) 25°C   (b) 50°C   (c) 75°C   (d) 100°C

9. If one boils water it will convert into ....
   (a) mist   (b) steam   (c) clouds   (d) snow

10. When you push something, you apply ....
    (a) force   (b) acceleration   (c) mass   (d) compression

11. Which material from the following has the highest transparency?
    (a) Paper   (b) Wood   (c) Metal   (d) Glass

12. Name the first and last colour of rainbow.

    (a) Blue and White   (b) Yellow and Violet   (c) Violet and Red   (d) Green and Red

13. The mirror that we use in our dressing table or home is known as ....
    (a) plane mirror   (b) concave mirror   (c) convex mirror   (d) None of these

14. .... and .... are solid form of water.
    (a) Snow, cold water   (b) Steam, ice   (c) Snow, ice   (d) None of these

15. Why do wooden blocks float on the water?
    (a) Because they are less denser than water.   (b) Because they are more denser than water.
    (c) Because we can make boat of wood.   (d) None of these

16. Name the device that is shown in the image.

    (a) Thermometer   (b) Stethoscope   (c) MRI machine   (d) None of these

17. LED stands for ....
    (a) Light Emitting Diode   (b) Light Emitter Diode
    (c) Light Enter Device   (d) Lamp Emitting Device

18. Find the correct food chain from the following options.
    (a) Deer —— Lion —— Snake   (b) Grass —— Deer —— Lion
    (c) Grass —— Lion —— Deer   (d) Deer —— Grass —— Lion

19. What is the normal human body temperature?
    (a) 98.6 F (approx)   (b) 97.2 (approx)   (c) 95.8 F (approx)   (d) 93.2 F (approx)

20. The pencil that we use are made up of .... and ....
    (a) wood, silver   (b) iron, wood   (c) wood, graphite   (d) copper, silver

Chapter 11

Computers

1. In CPU 'P' stands for ....
   (a) processing   (b) power
   (c) point   (d) None of these

2. .... is known as the father of computers.
   (a) Charles Babbage   (b) Douglas Englebart
   (c) Alan Turnig   (d) Clifford Berry

3. What do we call a computer that fits on a desk and is meant to stay at one location?
   (a) Monitor   (b) Laptop   (c) Desktop   (d) Palmtop

4. .... is a device used to provide visual output from a computer.
   (a) CPU   (b) Mouse
   (c) Keyboard   (d) Monitor

5. Name the device that is used to enter characters into computer system by pressing keys or buttons.
   (a) Monitor   (b) Keyboard
   (c) Mouse   (d) Desktop

6. Name the device that is used to print the documents from the computer.
   (a) Monitor   (b) CPU   (c) Mouse   (d) Printer

7. 'DVD' stands for ....
   (a) Digital Versatile Disc   (b) Digital Video Drive
   (c) Domain Virtual Drive   (d) Digital Video Domain

8. .... maintains power to the connected devices of a computer when power gets disconnected.
   (a) Central Processing Unit (CPU)   (b) Monitor
   (c) IC Chips   (d) UPS

9. Which of the following is not a Web Browser?
   (a) Windows Explorer   (b) Google Chrome
   (c) Internet Explorer   (d) Mozilla Firefox

10. Match the following.

	List I		List II
A.	Mouse	1.	Type letters and numbers
B.	Keyboard	2.	Display information
C.	Monitor	3.	Backup power
D.	UPS	4.	Point anything on screen

Codes

	A	B	C	D			A	B	C	D
(a)	2	3	1	4		(b)	4	1	2	3
(c)	1	2	4	3		(d)	4	2	1	3

11. Which of the following devices is used to store information permanently?

(a) Printer   (b) Mouse   (c) Keyboard   (d) Hark Disk

12. You can record your voice or other sounds into the computer when you speak over a
....

(a) Headphone   (b) Speaker
(c) Microphone   (d) None of these

13. Which of the following is an input device?

(a) Printer   (b) Monitor   (c) Speakers   (d) Keyboard

14. 'Monitor' is an .... device.

(a) input   (b) output   (c) CPU   (d) sound card

15. Select the processing device from the following options.

(a) Motherboard   (b) Monitor
(c) Printer   (d) Keyboard

16. Select the wrong match from the following options.

(a) Keyboard – Input device   (b) Printer – Output device
(c) Mouse – Processing device   (d) None of these

17. Pick the odd one out.

(a) Facebook   (b) Google Chrome   (c) Whatsapp   (d) Instagram

18. Which of the following protects our computer from virus?

(a) Antivirus software   (b) Malware
(c) Web Browser   (d) CD Drive

19. Which key is used to write alphabets in capital letters from a keyboard?

(a) Num lock key   (b) Enter key   (c) Caps lock key   (d) Home key

20. Pick the odd one out.

(a) Monitor   (b) Mouse   (c) Keyboard   (d) Charger

Chapter 12

Space Science

1. 'NASA' stands for ....
    (a) National Aeronautics and Space Administration
    (b) Narcotics Aeronautics and Space Administration
    (c) Night Aeronautics and Space Administration
    (d) National Aerospace and Space Administration

2. Name the woman astronaut who has the record for the most spacewalk.
    (a) Kalpana Chawla   (b) Sunita Williams
    (c) Eileen Collins   (d) Rakesh Sharma

3. Name the vehicle through which astronauts go to the space.
    (a) Spacecraft   (b) Aeroplane
    (c) UFO   (d) None of these

4. 'ISRO' stands for ....
    (a) Indian Space Research Organisation   (b) India Space Researcher Organisation
    (c) Indian Scientist Research Organisation (d) Indian Space Research Organiser

5. The person who goes to space for different space missions is known as ....
    (a) pilot   (b) astronaut
    (c) driver   (d) None of these

6. The space research agency of Japan is known as ....
    (a) DRDO   (b) BHEL
    (c) JAXA   (d) NASA

7. 'NASA' is a federal government space agency of which country?
    (a) United Kingdom   (b) United States of America
    (c) India   (d) Russia

8. .... is the second lunar (Moon) exploration mission developed by ISRO.
    (a) Chandrayaan-2   (b) Chandrayaan-1
    (c) Chandrayaan-3   (d) None of these

9. Name the instrument that is mainly used by astronomers to see the stars.
   - (a) Telescope
   - (b) Magnifying glass
   - (c) Mirror
   - (d) Microscope

10. Name the first Indian origin woman to go in the space.
    - (a) Kalpana Chawla
    - (b) Kiran Bedi
    - (c) Sunita Williams
    - (d) None of these

11. Which of the following is a space transportation service company?
    - (a) ISRO
    - (b) DRDO
    - (c) NASA
    - (d) SpaceEx

12. India has sent which space mission to study the Moon?
    - (a) Aditya
    - (b) Mangalyan
    - (c) Chandrayaan
    - (d) Vajrayan

13. Who is known as the father of 'Indian Space Programme'?
    - (a) Albert Einstein
    - (b) K. Sivan
    - (c) Vikram Sarabhai
    - (d) C.V. Raman

14. Which of the following craft or vehicle is not used in space mission?

    (a)

    (b)

    (c)

    (d) None of these

15. Mars Orbiter Mission is also known as ....
    - (a) Mangalyaan
    - (b) Chandrayaan
    - (c) Suryayaan
    - (d) None of these

Largest and Smallest

1. Name the tallest building in the world.
   - (a) Burj Khalifa, UAE
   - (b) Shanghai Tower
   - (c) Qutub Minar
   - (d) Leaning Tower of Pisa

2. Which is the highest mountain peak in the world?
   - (a) K2
   - (b) Mount Everest
   - (c) Alps
   - (d) Mount Kilimanjaro

3. Which is the tallest animal in the world?
   - (a) African Elephant
   - (b) Saltwater Crocodile
   - (c) Giraffe
   - (d) Bear

4. Name the longest river in the world.
   - (a) Ganga
   - (b) Nile
   - (c) Amazon
   - (d) Mississippi

5. Which is the biggest and deepest ocean in the world?
   - (a) Pacific Ocean
   - (b) Indian Ocean
   - (c) Atlantic Ocean
   - (d) Arctic Ocean

6. Which is the smallest bird in the world?
   - (a) Sparrow
   - (b) Humming bird
   - (c) Pigeon
   - (d) Parrot

7. Which is the smallest planet in our solar system?
   - (a) Earth
   - (b) Venus
   - (c) Uranus
   - (d) Mercury

8. Which is the longest dam in India?
   - (a) Hirakud Dam
   - (b) Tehri Dam
   - (c) Sardar Sarovar Dam
   - (d) None of these

9. Which is the smallest country in the world?
   - (a) China
   - (b) Uganda
   - (c) Vatican City
   - (d) France

10. Which is the longest river of India?
    (a) Krishna river
    (b) Ganga river
    (c) Godavari river
    (d) Narmada river

11. Which is the highest dam in India?
    (a) Tehri Dam (260 meters)
    (b) Bhakra Dam (225.55 meters)
    (c) Hirakud Dam (61 meters)
    (d) Sardar Sarovar Dam (138.68 meters)

12. Which is the largest lake in the world?
    (a) Lake Victoria (Area 68,800 km^2)
    (b) Lake Superior (Area 82,103 km^2)
    (c) Lake Huron (Area 59,600 km^2)
    (d) Caspian Sea (Area 371,000 km^2)

13. Which is the largest cricket stadium of the world?
    (a) The Oval, England
    (b) The Gabba, Australia
    (c) Narendra Modi Stadium, India
    (d) Ram Nath Kovind Stadium, India

14. Which is the highest waterfall in the world?
    (a) Yosemite Falls (California, USA)
    (b) Angel Falls (Venezuela, South America)
    (c) Niagara Falls (USA and Canada, North America)
    (d) Victoria Falls (Zimbabwe, Africa)

15. Which is the world's tallest monument?
    (a) Gateway Arch (USA)
    (b) Qutub Minar (New Delhi, India)
    (c) Eiffel Tower (Paris, France)
    (d) The Empire State Building (New York City, USA)

16. Which is the smallest state of India by area?
    (a) Kerala
    (b) Goa
    (c) Manipur
    (d) Tripura

17. Which is the largest island of the world?
    (a) Iceland
    (b) Greenland
    (c) Andaman and Nicobar Islands
    (d) Island

18. Which is the largest desert of the world?
    (a) Gobi Desert
    (b) Thar Desert
    (c) Sonoran Desert
    (d) Sahara Desert

19. Which is the largest Mosque in India?
    (a) Mecca Masjid, Hyderabad
    (b) Taj-ul Masjid, Bhopal
    (c) Jama Masjid, New Delhi
    (d) Bara Imambara, Lucknow

20. Name the largest country of the world in terms of area.
    (a) China
    (b) United States of America
    (c) India
    (d) Russia

Chapter 14

Books and Authors

1. Who is the author of 'Ramayan'?
   (a) Kabir Das
   (b) Valmiki
   (c) Rahim
   (d) None of these

2. Arjun, Bhima, Nakul, Sehdev are famous characters of which book?
   (a) Ramayan
   (b) Mahabharata
   (c) Veda
   (d) None of these

3. Which of the books is a story of a child who is a wizard studying in Hogwarts school?
   (a) Charlie and the Chocolate Factory
   (b) Harry Potter
   (c) Jumanji
   (d) None of these

4. Who is the author of 'Gitanjali'?
   (a) Chetan Bhagat
   (b) Rabindranath Tagore
   (c) Ramnath Kovind
   (d) None of these

5. God 'Jesus' is related to which holy book?
   (a) Bible
   (b) Quran
   (c) Ramayan
   (d) Geeta

6. Which novel has the famous character Mogli?
   (a) Harry Potter
   (b) Oliver Twist
   (c) Jungle Book
   (d) Popeye the Sailor

7. Who is the author of 'Discovery of India'?
   (a) Mahatma Gandhi
   (b) Narendra Modi
   (c) Shivaji Maharaj
   (d) Jawaharlal Nehru

8. Who is the author of 'Mahabharat'?
   (a) Veda Vyasa
   (b) Valmiki
   (c) Surdas
   (d) Kabir

9. Who is the author of the novel 'Malgudi Days'?
   - (a) R.K. Narayan
   - (b) APJ Abdul Kalam
   - (c) Ruskin Bond
   - (d) Subhash Chandra Bose

10. Which of these character is found in the stories of Arabian Nights?
   - (a) Harry
   - (b) Dholu
   - (c) Bheem
   - (d) Aladin

11. The famous novel 'Three Mistakes of My Life' is written by
   - (a) Vikram Seth
   - (b) Chetan Bhagat
   - (c) R.K. Narayan
   - (d) Ruskin Bond

12. Name the language in which four 'Vedas' are written.
   - (a) Sanskrit
   - (b) Hindi
   - (c) English
   - (d) Urdu

13. Who is the author of 'Panchatantra'?
   - (a) Pandit Vishnu Sharma
   - (b) Harivansh Rai Bachchan
   - (c) M.K. Gandhi
   - (d) None of these

14. The famous hindi novel Godan is written by
   - (a) Harivansh Rai Bachan
   - (b) Premchand
   - (c) Mahadevi Verma
   - (d) Kabirdas

15. 'Guru Granth Sahib' is related to which religion?
   - (a) Buddhism
   - (b) Islam
   - (c) Sikhism
   - (d) Jainism

Important Days and Dates

1. Which day is celebrated as Children's Day in India?
   (a) 15th August
   (b) 2nd October
   (c) 26th January
   (d) 14th November

2. .... is celebrated as International Day of Yoga.
   (a) 21st June
   (b) 22nd June
   (c) 21st May
   (d) 22nd May

3. .... is celebrated as Indian Army Day.
   (a) 15th January of every year
   (b) 16th March of every year
   (c) 14th January of every year
   (d) 17th January of every year

4. Which of the following day is celebrated in the month of January?
   (a) Independence Day
   (b) Gandhi Jayanti
   (c) Teacher's Day
   (d) Republic Day

5. On every .... Prime Minister of India addresses the nation on occasion of Independence Day.
   (a) 26th January
   (b) 15th August
   (c) 20th January
   (d) 12th May

6. 8th October, of every year is celebrated as ....
   (a) Indian Army Day
   (b) Indian Navy Day
   (c) Indian Airforce Day
   (d) None of these

7. International Women's Day is celebrated on ....
   (a) 1st February
   (b) 2nd October
   (c) 5th May
   (d) 8th March

8. Dr. Sarvepalli Radhakrishnan's (Former President of India) birthday is celebrated on ....
    (a) 5th September   (b) 10th August
    (c) 15th August   (d) 31st October

9. 2nd October is celebrated as birth anniversary of ....
    (a) Father of Nation   (b) Iron Man of India
    (c) Subhash Chandra Bose   (d) Dr. Rajendra Prasad

10. Friendship Day is celebrated on which date?
    (a) 1st January   (b) 1st August
    (c) 25th December   (d) 2nd February

11. 22nd March is celebrated as ....
    (a) World Water Day   (b) World Health Day
    (c) World Environment Day   (d) Republic Day

12. Hindi Day is celebrated on
    (a) 14th September   (b) 15th August
    (c) 25th December   (d) None of these

13. Christmas Day is celebrated on
    (a) 25th December   (b) 26th December
    (c) 27th December   (d) 24th December

14. Match the following.

Days	Dates
A. Father's Day	1. 2nd Sunday of May
B. National Sports Day	2. 3rd Sunday of June
C. Mother's Day	3. 29th August

Codes

     A   B   C   A   B   C
(a) 1   3   2   (b) 2   3   1
(c) 3   2   1   (d) None of these

15. Which of these two festivals are celebrated on same day?
    (a) Makar Sankranti, Diwali   (b) Makar Sankranti, Pongal
    (c) Makar Sankranti, Lohri   (d) None of these

Chapter 16

Sports

1. 'Punch' term is related to which game?
   (a) Baseball
   (b) Boxing
   (c) Cricket
   (d) Football

2. Which out of the following terms is related to 'Chess'?
   (a) Baseball
   (b) Lawn Tennis
   (c) Badminton
   (d) Checkmate

3. 'Hat-trick' term is related to which game?
   (a) Football
   (b) Kabaddi
   (c) Cricket
   (d) None of these

4. 'Goal' term is mostly used in which sport?
   (a) Football
   (b) Tennis
   (c) Cricket
   (d) Badminton

5. Which out of the following terms is related to 'Karate'?
   (a) Kick
   (b) Goal
   (c) Checkmate
   (d) Out

6. From the given options, count how many games are not indoor?

   Football, Basketball, Cricket, Carrom, Chess, Rugby, Baseball, Kabaddi, Kho-Kho, Volleyball
   (a) 8
   (b) 7
   (c) 5
   (d) 4

7. Chess : Indoors :: .... : Outdoors.
   (a) Cricket
   (b) Carrom
   (c) Cards
   (d) None of these

8. Cricket is played on which of the following?
   (a) Court
   (b) Ring
   (c) Rink
   (d) Pitch

9. Match the following games with their playing areas.

Game		Playing Area	
A.	Badminton	1.	Square board
B.	Boxing	2.	Court
C.	Chess	3.	Ring

Codes

    A B C   A B C

(a) 2 3 1   (b) 1 3 2

(c) 2 1 3   (d) None of these

10. Which one of the following is not played in Ring?
(a) Boxing
(b) Wrestling
(c) Golf
(d) None of these

11. Which one of the following is not related to Cricket?
(a) Virat Kohli
(b) Sachin Tendulkar
(c) Usain Bolt
(d) Rohit Sharma

12. Famous player Mohammad Ali is related with which sports?
(a) Boxing
(b) Wrestling
(c) Weightlifting
(d) Archery

13. Cricket is known as the 'National Game' of ....
(a) Australia
(b) Russia
(c) Pakistan
(d) United States of America

14. The logo shown in the image below represents which international sports committtee.

(a) Commonwealth games
(b) Asian games
(c) Olympic games
(d) None of these

15. Identify the sport symbol shown in the given image.

(a) Baseball (b) Cricket
(c) Football (d) Cycling

16. Identify the sport symbol shown in the image.

(a) Football (b) Cricket (c) Cycling (d) Golf

17. The equipment shown in the image is related to which game?

(a) Cricket (b) Golf (c) Snooker (d) Chess

18. In the given image, what is cricket umpire signalling?

(a) 4 runs (b) 6 runs (c) Out (d) No ball

19. Identify the player shown in the image.

(a) Virat Kohli   (b) Rohit Sharma
(c) M.S. Dhoni   (d) Sachin Tendulkar

20. Name the woman who is the first Indian to win a medal in Badminton at the Olympics.

(a) Saina Nehwal   (b) P.V. Sindhu
(c) P.T. Usha   (d) Sakshi Malik

21. Which of these footballers has been the captain of Indian National Football Team?
(a) Neeraj Chopra   (b) Sardara Singh
(c) Sunil Chettri   (d) Kapil Dev

22. Which one of the following players belongs to Haryana?
(a) Geeta Phogat   (b) Mary Kom
(c) M.S. Dhoni   (d) Sachin Tendulkar

23. Name the player shown in the image.

(a) Saina Nehwal   (b) Sania Mirza
(c) P.V. Sindhu   (d) Geeta Phogat

24. Which of the following boxer has won an olympic medal for India?
    (a) Abhinav Bindra
    (b) Sushil Kumar
    (c) Vijendar Singh
    (d) Gagan Narang

25. Which Indian athlete is known as 'Flying Sikh'?
    (a) Milkha Singh
    (b) P.T. Usha
    (c) Virat Kohli
    (d) Major Dhyanchandra

26. Identify the player shown in the image.

    (a) Rahul Dravid
    (b) Sunil Gavaskar
    (c) Kapil Dev
    (d) None of these

27. Identify the player shown in the image.

    (a) Rohit Sharma
    (b) Virat Kohli
    (c) Shikhar Dhawan
    (d) M.S. Dhoni

Chapter 17

Current Affairs

1. Which of the following is the newest Union Territory of India?
   (a) Andaman and Nicobar
   (b) Ladakh
   (c) Chandigarh
   (d) Lakshadweep

2. Which mission has been started by India to bring back Indian citizens from foreign countries trapped due to COVID-19?
   (a) Bharat Mata Mission
   (b) Jai Jawan Mission
   (c) Cowin Mission
   (d) Vande Bharat Mission

3. What is the name of ISRO's new humanoid robot that will go to space next?
   (a) Pragyan
   (b) Jagjivan
   (c) Vyommitra
   (d) Manav

4. Statue of Peace was inaugurated by Prime Minister in which state?
   (a) Madhya Pradesh
   (b) Haryana
   (c) Rajasthan
   (d) Bihar

5. What is the name of world's longest highway tunnel, inaugurated in India in 2020?
   (a) Jawahar Tunnel
   (b) Atal Tunnel
   (c) Mahatma Tunnel
   (d) Buddha Tunnel

6. Who among the following is the current (2021) President of the United States of America?
   (a) Barack Obama
   (b) Donald Trump
   (c) Joe Biden
   (d) Kamla Harris

7. Sputnik-V Corona Vaccine belongs to which country?
   (a) Canada
   (b) Brazil
   (c) Russia
   (d) Japan

8. The Rafael Jet fighter aircraft has been bought from which country?
   (a) Dubai
   (b) France
   (c) China
   (d) America

9. Who has won the Dadasaheb Phalke Award in 2021?
   (a) Rekha
   (b) Rajnikanth
   (c) Abhishek Bachan
   (d) Salman Khan

10. The largest Tulip garden of Asia has been opened in ....
    (a) China
    (b) Bhutan
    (c) India
    (d) Myanmar

PRACTICE SET 01

1. The National Park that was the first tiger reserve in India is............. .
   (a) Gir National Park
   (b) Sundarban National Park
   (c) Jim Corbett National Park
   (d) Kanha National Park

2. Which of the following organ is part of the circulatory system?
   (a) Lungs
   (b) Kidneys
   (c) Heart
   (d) Liver

3. Jana-Gana-Mana was originally composed in............. .
   (a) Gujarati
   (b) Hindi
   (c) Bengali
   (d) Marathi

4. People of which religious group worship at the place known as Fire Temple?
   (a) Sikhs
   (b) Muslims
   (c) Parsis
   (d) Christians

5. Statement 1 Independence Day of India is celebrated on 12th August of every year.
   Statement 2 Repulic Day of India is celebrated on 26th January of every year.
   (a) Statement 1 is correct
   (b) Statement 2 is correct
   (c) Both Statements are correct
   (d) Both Statements are incorrect

6. Saffron colour in the National Flag of India represents ....
   (a) peace and truth
   (b) strength and courage
   (c) growth and auspiciousness of the land
   (d) None of these

7. Which dance is being practised in the image shown below?

   (a) Bharatnatyam
   (b) Kathak
   (c) Lavani
   (d) Garba

8. Who was the first man from India to go into space?
   (a) Raja Chari
   (b) Rakesh Sharma
   (c) C.V. Raman
   (d) Ramanujam

9. 'Sunlight' is a good source of which vitamin?
   (a) Vitamin A
   (b) Vitamin B12
   (c) Vitamin D
   (d) Vitamin E

10. The famous Taj Mahal Hotel is located in which city?
    (a) Chandigarh
    (b) Mumbai
    (c) Chennai
    (d) Kochi

11. 'ROM' stands for ....
    (a) Read Only Memory
    (b) Read One Memory
    (c) Read Only Messages
    (d) Read Once Memory

12. Name the first woman President of India.
    (a) Kiran Bedi
    (b) Kiran Majumdar Shaw
    (c) Pratibha Patil
    (d) None of these

13. National Calendar of India is............. .
    (a) Gregorian Calendar
    (b) Vikram Samvat Calendar
    (c) Hindu Calendar
    (d) Saka Calendar

14. The flag shown in the image is of which country?

    (a) USA
    (b) Iran
    (c) India
    (d) Pakistan

15. What is the ratio of width of our National Flag to its length?
    (a) 1 : 2
    (b) 2 : 3
    (c) 3 : 4
    (d) 1 : 4

16. .... is the common capital of Punjab and Haryana.
    (a) Lucknow
    (b) Chandigarh
    (c) Patna
    (d) Ranchi

17. Identify the sport being played in the picture

(a) Hockey   (b) Golf   (c) Polo   (d) Cricket

18. Which of the following components are major nutrients in our food?
(a) Carbohydrates   (b) Lipids and Proteins
(c) Vitamins and Minerals   (d) All of these

19. Find the wrong match from the following options.
(a) Water Transport – Cargo Ship   (b) Air Transport – Boeing 747
(c) Land Transport – Submarine   (d) Rail Transport – Shatabdi Express

20. Name the place where Republic Day parade takes place.
(a) Agra   (b) Red Fort
(c) Rajpath   (d) None of these

21. India became a Republic nation on ....
(a) 15th August, 1947   (b) 26th January, 1950
(c) 3rd September, 193   (d) 30th January, 1948

22. Which is the smallest continent?
(a) Africa   (b) Asia
(c) Australia   (d) Europe

23. Name the capital of Bangladesh.
(a) Delhi   (b) Islamabad   (c) Tokyo   (d) Dhaka

24. 'Knock out' term is mostly used in which sport?
(a) Boxing   (b) Tennis   (c) Cricket   (d) Badminton

25. Name the planet which is known as 'twin planet' of Earth.
(a) Venus   (b) Mars   (c) Saturn   (d) Jupiter

26. Which of these means of communication is used to travel to other countries?
(a) Air Transport   (b) Roadways
(c) Animal Transport   (d) Railways

27. Find the incorrect statement.
    (a) We breathe faster when we run.   (b) Kidneys are located in our skull.
    (c) We have two eyes.   (d) All of these

28. Which of the following mineral is helpful in keeping our teeth strong?
    (a) Iron   (b) Copper   (c) Calcium   (d) None of these

29. Hockey : Outdoors : : ....: Indoors.
    (a) Football   (b) Cricket   (c) Basketball   (d) Chess

30. Name the National currency of United States of America.
    (a) Riyal   (b) Rupee   (c) Dinar   (d) Dollar

31. Which of the following is not a stringed instrument?
    (a) Sitar   (b) Guitar
    (c) Harmonium   (d) Harp

32. Which sports person is shown in the image given below?
    Hint: She has won an Olympic medal for India in wrestling

    (a) Hima Das   (b) Sakshi Malik
    (c) Mary Kom   (d) Deepa Karmakar

33. Dark rain clouds can give out lightning and ....
    (a) thunder   (b) snow
    (c) sunlight   (d) wind

34. Name the tallest statue of India.
    (a) Statue of Liberty   (b) Statue of Friendship
    (c) Statue of Buddha   (d) Statue of Unity

35. In which year did the Quit India Movement start?
    (a) 1945   (b) 1930
    (c) 1939   (d) 1942

1. What is the National currency of United Kingdom?
   (a) Dollar   (b) Pound   (c) Dirham   (d) Rupee

2. Who is the writer of the popular story-Swami and Friends?
   (a) Premchand   (b) R.K. Narayan
   (c) Chetan Bhagat   (d) A.P.J. Abdul Kalam

3. Match the following.

	List I		List II
A.	Earth	1.	Second largest planet
B.	Saturn	2.	Nearest planet to Sun
C.	Neptune	3.	Only planet where life exist
D.	Mercury	4.	Farthest planet to Sun

   Codes

	A	B	C	D			A	B	C	D
(a)	3	1	2	4		(b)	1	3	4	2
(c)	3	1	4	2		(d)	None of these			

4. The image given below is

   (a) National Statue of India   (b) National Emblem of India
   (c) National Bird of India   (d) None of these

5. Which leader gave the slogan 'Jai Hind'?
   (a) Mahatma Gandhi   (b) Lal Bahadur Shastri
   (c) Subhash Chandra Bose   (d) Bhagat Singh

6. Which freedom fighter was hanged to death by the British Government at very young age?
   (a) Bhagat Singh
   (b) Subhash Chandra Bose
   (c) Mahatma Gandhi
   (d) None of these

7. Kabul is capital of which country?
   (a) Bangladesh   (b) India   (c) Afghanistan   (d) None of these

8. Which of the following is not a National festival of India?
   (a) Diwali   (b) Holi   (c) Independence Day   (d) Gudi Padwa

9. Name the founder of Tata industries.
   (a) Jamshetji Tata
   (b) Ratan Tata
   (c) JRD Tata
   (d) Ratanji Dadabhoy Tata

10. Which system does lungs belong to?
    (a) Digestive system
    (b) Respiratory system
    (c) Circulatory system
    (d) Excretory system

11. Match the following.

List I	List II
A. System Software	1. Pen Drive
B. Application	2. Window 7
C. Storage Device	3. Microsoft Office

Codes

    A   D   C   A   B   C
(a) 2   3   1   (b) 3   1   2
(c) 2   1   3   (d) None of these

12. Which phenomenon results in day and night on Earth?
    (a) Rotation
    (b) Revolution
    (c) The orbit of the Earth
    (d) When the Moon blocks the Sun

13. Name the person who has created Mickey Mouse.
    (a) Rudyard Kipling   (b) Albert Einstein   (c) Walt Disney   (d) Walt Mickey

14. The Birth Aniversary of Jesus is celebrated on which day by the Christian people?
    (a) Mahaveer Jayanti
    (b) Easter
    (c) Christmas
    (d) Diwali

15. Identify the person shown in the image, he is the former President of 'South Africa'.

(a) Bill Gates   (b) Joe Biden
(c) Martin Luther King   (d) Nelson Mandela

16. Who is the author of 'Jungle Book'?
(a) Rudyard Kipling   (b) Walt Disney
(c) Harish Salve   (d) Barack Obama

17. Who is the chief architect of the Indian Constitution?
(a) Bhimrao Ambedkar   (b) Sardar Vallabhbhai Patel
(c) Abul Kalam Azad   (d) Jawaharlal Nehru

18. Rome is the capital of which country of world?
(a) Singapore   (b) Pakistan   (c) Turkey   (d) Italy

19. Identify the name of the country from the given flag.

(a) Pakistan   (b) China
(c) America   (d) None of these

20. Which city is known as the city of Pearls?
(a) Chennai   (b) Mumbai   (c) Hyderabad   (d) Delhi

21. The name of first mission to moon, launched by USA was
(a) Moon Mission   (b) Apollo Mission
(c) Light Mission   (d) Rocket Mission

22. Identify the Indian cricketer shown in the image.

(a) Mohammad Shami   (b) Ishant Sharma

(c) Rohit Sharma   (d) Yuzvendra Chahal

23. 8th October of every year is celebrated as ....

(a) Indian Army Day   (b) Indian Navy Day

(c) Indian Airforce Day   (d) None of these

24. Name the monument from which Prime Minister addresses the nation on Independence Day.

(a) Taj Mahal   (b) Red Fort   (c) Indian Parliament   (d) Agra Fort

25. .... is the lunar (Moon) exploration mission developed by ISRO.

(a) Chandrayaan   (b) Mangalyaan   (c) Suryayaan   (d) None of these

26. Which of these items is not produced from milk?

(a) Cheese   (b) Curd   (c) Butter   (d) Corn

27. Which is the longest river of India?

(a) Ganga   (b) Krishna   (c) Godavari   (d) Yamuna

28. Match the following.

List I	List II
A. Respiratory System	1. Bones
B. Skeletal System	2. Mouth, Foodpipe, Stomach
C. Digestive System	3. Lungs, Windpipe

Codes

	A	B	C			A	B	C
(a)	2	1	3		(b)	1	3	2
(c)	3	1	2		(d)	None of these		

29. The gas which is present in largest quantity on Earth is.............. .
    (a) Hydrogen   (b) Oxygen
    (c) Nitrogen   (d) Carbon Dioxide

30. Which of the following is not correctly matched?
    (a) Arvind Kejriwal — Politician   (b) Sunidhi Chauhan — Singer
    (c) R.K. Narayan — Novelist   (d) Ravindra Jadeja — Dancer

31. Raj Ghat, the Samadhi of Mahatma Gandhi is in which city?
    (a) Dehradun   (b) Mumbai
    (c) Kolkata   (d) Delhi

32. Vitamin A, necessary for a good eyesight is found in which of these food?
    (a) Banana   (b) Milk
    (c) Eggs   (d) Both (b) and (c)

33. Which one of the following is not played in Ring?
    (a) Boxing   (b) Wrestling
    (c) Golf   (d) None of these

34. Which of the following is a human-powered transport?
    (a) Bullock cart   (b) Yacht
    (c) Rickshaw   (d) Ambulance

35. .... is composed of molten rocks that comes out during a volcanic eruption.
    (a) Magma   (b) Lava
    (c) Crust   (d) Core

Answers

Chapter 1   Solar System

1. (d)	**2.** (d)	**3.** (c)	**4.** (d)	**5.** (c)	**6.** (a)	**7.** (d)	**8.** (d)	**9.** (d)	**10.** (c)
11. (b)	**12.** (c)	**13.** (c)	**14.** (c)	**15.** (c)	**16.** (b)	**17.** (a)	**18.** (c)	**19.** (c)	**20.** (b)
21. (d)	**22.** (c)	**23.** (b)	**24.** (b)	**25.** (c)	**26.** (b)	**27.** (d)	**28.** (a)	**29.** (d)	**30.** (a)
31. (b)	**32.** (b)	**33.** (b)	**34.** (d)						

Chapter 2   My Country

1. (b)	**2.** (d)	**3.** (d)	**4.** (d)	**5.** (b)	**6.** (d)	**7.** (c)	**8.** (b)	**9.** (c)	**10.** (c)
11. (b)	**12.** (d)	**13.** (d)	**14.** (c)	**15.** (c)	**16.** (a)	**17.** (c)	**18.** (a)	**19.** (d)	**20.** (d)

Chapter 3   Countries of the World

1. (d)	**2.** (a)	**3.** (a)	**4.** (c)	**5.** (d)	**6.** (c)	**7.** (d)	**8.** (b)	**9.** (c)	**10.** (c)
11. (a)	**12.** (b)	**13.** (a)	**14.** (d)	**15.** (d)	**16.** (d)	**17.** (b)	**18.** (d)	**19.** (a)	**20.** (a)
21. (a)	**22.** (a)	**23.** (c)	**24.** (b)	**25.** (c)	**26.** (c)	**27.** (d)	**28.** (d)		

Chapter 4   Music and Dance

1. (d)	**2.** (c)	**3.** (a)	**4.** (d)	**5.** (d)	**6.** (c)	**7.** (a)	**8.** (b)	**9.** (c)	**10.** (c)
11. (a)	**12.** (a)	**13.** (b)	**14.** (d)	**15.** (a)	**16.** (b)	**17.** (b)	**18.** (d)	**19.** (d)	**20.** (b)
21. (a)									

Chapter 5   Transport and Communication

1. (a)	**2.** (c)	**3.** (c)	**4.** (a)	**5.** (d)	**6.** (d)	**7.** (d)	**8.** (d)	**9.** (d)	**10.** (d)
11. (a)	**12.** (d)	**13.** (c)	**14.** (c)	**15.** (c)	**16.** (b)	**17.** (a)	**18.** (c)	**19.** (d)	**20.** (b)
21. (c)	**22.** (b)								

Chapter 6   Famous Places

1. (a)	**2.** (a)	**3.** (b)	**4.** (b)	**5.** (b)	**6.** (d)	**7.** (c)	**8.** (c)	**9.** (c)	**10.** (a)
11. (b)	**12.** (b)	**13.** (d)	**14.** (c)	**15.** (a)	**16.** (d)	**17.** (c)	**18.** (a)	**19.** (b)	**20.** (a)
21. (b)	**22.** (a)	**23.** (a)	**24.** (a)						

Chapter 7   National Personalities

1. (b)	**2.** (a)	**3.** (c)	**4.** (b)	**5.** (b)	**6.** (a)	**7.** (a)	**8.** (a)	**9.** (b)	**10.** (c)
11. (c)	**12.** (b)	**13.** (c)	**14.** (a)	**15.** (d)	**16.** (d)	**17.** (c)	**18.** (c)	**19.** (a)	

Chapter 8   Human Body

1. (a)	2. (c)	3. (c)	4. (a)	5. (b)	6. (b)	7. (d)	8. (b)	9. (c)	10. (a)
11. (d)	12. (d)	13. (a)	14. (b)	15. (b)	16. (d)	17. (d)	18. (a)	19. (c)	20. (b)
21. (c)	22. (b)	23. (c)	24. (c)	25. (c)	26. (a)	27. (c)	28. (b)	29. (b)	30. (d)

Chapter 9   Food and Nutrition

1. (d)	2. (d)	3. (b)	4. (d)	5. (b)	6. (d)	7. (c)	8. (b)	9. (c)	10. (c)
11. (b)	12. (d)	13. (a)	14. (b)	15. (b)	16. (b)	17. (d)	18. (d)	19. (a)	20. (a)
21. (c)									

Chapter 10   Everyday Science

1. (a)	2. (a)	3. (a)	4. (c)	5. (c)	6. (a)	7. (a)	8. (d)	9. (b)	10. (a)
11. (d)	12. (c)	13. (a)	14. (c)	15. (a)	16. (b)	17. (a)	18. (b)	19. (a)	20. (c)

Chapter 11   Computers

1. (a)	2. (a)	3. (c)	4. (d)	5. (b)	6. (d)	7. (a)	8. (d)	9. (a)	10. (b)
11. (d)	12. (c)	13. (d)	14. (b)	15. (a)	16. (c)	17. (b)	18. (a)	19. (c)	20. (d)

Chapter 12   Space Science

1. (a)	2. (b)	3. (a)	4. (a)	5. (b)	6. (c)	7. (b)	8. (a)	9. (a)	10. (a)
11. (d)	12. (c)	13. (c)	14. (a)	15. (a)					

Chapter 13   Largest and Smallest

1. (a)	2. (b)	3. (c)	4. (b)	5. (a)	6. (b)	7. (d)	8. (a)	9. (c)	10. (b)
11. (a)	12. (d)	13. (c)	14. (b)	15. (a)	16. (b)	17. (b)	18. (d)	19. (c)	20. (d)

Chapter 14   Books and Authors

1. (b)	2. (b)	3. (b)	4. (b)	5. (a)	6. (c)	7. (d)	8. (a)	9. (a)	10. (d)
11. (b)	12. (a)	13. (a)	14. (b)	15. (c)					

Chapter 15   Important Days and Dates

1. (d)	2. (a)	3. (a)	4. (d)	5. (b)	6. (c)	7. (d)	8. (a)	9. (a)	10. (b)
11. (a)	12. (a)	13. (a)	14. (b)	15. (b)					

Chapter 16 Sports

1. (b)	**2.** (d)	**3.** (c)	**4.** (a)	**5.** (a)	**6.** (a)	**7.** (a)	**8.** (d)	**9.** (a)	**10.** (c)
11. (c)	**12.** (a)	**13.** (a)	**14.** (c)	**15.** (d)	**16.** (a)	**17.** (c)	**18.** (b)	**19.** (a)	**20.** (a)
21. (c)	**22.** (a)	**23.** (c)	**24.** (c)	**25.** (a)	**26.** (c)	**27.** (a)			

Chapter 17 Current Affairs

1. (b)	**2.** (d)	**3.** (c)	**4.** (c)	**5.** (b)	**6.** (c)	**7.** (c)	**8.** (b)	**9.** (b)	**10.** (c)

Practice Set 1

1. (c)	**2.** (c)	**3.** (c)	**4.** (c)	**5.** (b)	**6.** (b)	**7.** (b)	**8.** (b)	**9.** (c)	**10.** (b)
11. (a)	**12.** (c)	**13.** (d)	**14.** (b)	**15.** (b)	**16.** (b)	**17.** (b)	**18.** (d)	**19.** (c)	**20.** (c)
21. (b)	**22.** (c)	**23.** (d)	**24.** (a)	**25.** (a)	**26.** (a)	**27.** (b)	**28.** (c)	**29.** (d)	**30.** (d)
31. (c)	**32.** (b)	**33.** (a)	**34.** (d)	**35.** (d)					

Practice Set 2

1. (b)	**2.** (b)	**3.** (c)	**4.** (b)	**5.** (c)	**6.** (a)	**7.** (c)	**8.** (d)	**9.** (a)	**10.** (b)
11. (a)	**12.** (a)	**13.** (c)	**14.** (c)	**15.** (d)	**16.** (a)	**17.** (a)	**18.** (d)	**19.** (b)	**20.** (c)
21. (b)	**22.** (b)	**23.** (c)	**24.** (b)	**25.** (a)	**26.** (d)	**27.** (a)	**28.** (c)	**29.** (c)	**30.** (d)
31. (d)	**32.** (d)	**33.** (c)	**34.** (c)	**35.** (b)